The Inside Story Of a Wine Label

A comprehensive guide and industry insider's perspective on all of the required and non-required items seen on U.S. wine labels.

This book is for those who like to think while they drink.

Ann Reynolds

ISBN   **978-1481859844**

Table of Contents

Information Required on Wine Labels: A History

Information *Not* Required on Wine Labels

Sample Label

This sample of a set (front and back) illustrates information often seen on wine labels.

The numbers next to each item correspond to the chapter in which the information is discussed.

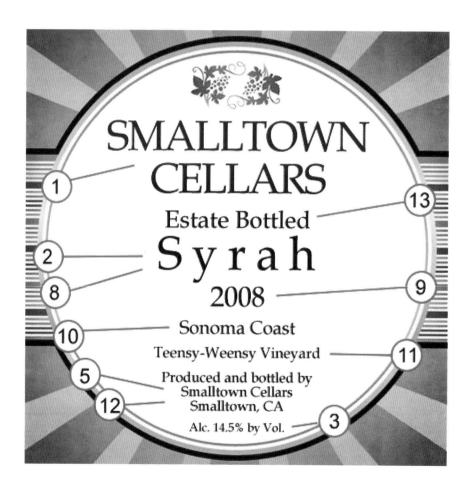

The story of Smalltown Cellars is one of a dream. The owners, Nathan and Mitilda Small, discovered a gorgeous piece of property 20 years ago, purchased it and began the process of making their dream a reality. This wine you're holding is the result of that dream and a genuine love of wine making. It was crafted with attention to detail accentuating the best qualities of the Syrah varietal with distinct notes of raspberries, currants and vanilla.

GOVERNMENT WARNING: (1) ACCORDING TO THE SURGEON GENERAL, WOMEN SHOULD NOT DRINK ALCOHOLIC BEVERAGES DURING PREGNANCY BECAUSE OF THE RISK OF BIRTH DEFECTS. (2) CONSUMPTION OF ALCOHOLIC BEVERAGES IMPAIRS YOUR ABILITY TO DRIVE OR OPERATE MACHINERY, AND MAY CAUSE HEALTH PROBLEMS.

CONTAINS SULFITES

750ml

Introduction

This book is a result of my over 20 year background in the wine industry, primarily in wine production. When I entered the world of winemaking, I only planned to work for a few months worth of a harvest season, and then go back to what I considered my "real job" — a full-time teaching position. But fate had a different plan. Years later, my teaching and wine careers collided as I realized the need for greater understanding about label compliance, and developed a college course on the subject. Now, as a teacher and wine professional, I'm on a mission to help consumers, connoisseurs and wine professionals understand what goes on a wine label and why.

Many people are surprised to learn the depth of information within wine labels. Labels serve as a display for the finished product of a wine's life. They function not only to draw in the consumer's attention, but also to tell the story about the wine itself. This book explains all of the information required to be on any U.S. wine label, and then explores many items we commonly see on labels that are not required. We will go into why winemakers sometimes fudge percentage requirements, and intricate government standards will be demystified. It is my guarantee that after reading this book, not only will you never look at a wine label the same way again, but you'll also enjoy a more informed and interactive wine shopping experience.

After working at several wineries over the past 15 years and being directly involved in the behind the scenes activity that goes into label design I decided to share some of my insights and experiences in the hopes of helping take your wine interactions to the next level. This book is my way of bringing you further inside the world of wine via the outside of the bottle. One of the ways I've done this is by sharing many of my own personal stories from over the years of interacting with all the behind the scenes activities that lead up to a label being placed on a bottle of wine and making its way to the store shelf.

The casual to savvy wine consumer can easily feel more in the know about a wine they are considering purchasing or one they are currently drinking simply by reading its label. Wine does not have to be complicated or intimidating and knowing what all those label details mean is one step towards simplifying them.

Information Required on Wine Labels: A History

Throughout United States history, the federal government has regulated the wine industry. Taxes were first imposed on alcohol in 1791 for the purpose of paying off the debt from the Revolutionary War. Wine first began being produced on a commercial basis in early 1800. Over time, the federal regulating agency gradually evolved into the Bureau of Alcohol, Tobacco and Firearms (BATF). Then in 2002, as a result of Congress passing the Homeland Security Act, guns graduated to a different agency, and the wine industry is now regulated by the Alcohol and Tobacco Tax and Trade Bureau, or TTB for short.

The TTB regulates all of the alcoholic beverage industry areas, which include distilled spirits, beer and wine. However when it comes to comparing the annual volumes each produces vs. the amount of label submissions each makes to the TTB the numbers are in opposite proportions. (Especially if you eliminate the volume that E & J Gallo contributes to the total, which is currently about 1/3) In other words the wine industry produces the smallest volume of the three (currently about 680 million gallons annually) but submits the largest amount of labels for approval. Label approval submissions from the wine industry make up over 80% of the total that the TTB receives, which for 2012 was over 145,000. I include this to give you a better idea of the large number of different wines on the market today. (But perhaps you had already noticed this from visiting the wine aisle at your local store!)

As part of their label approval process the TTB is looking for a specific set of mandatory information that must appear on all labels submitted. For wine, 11 items must appear, as seen below. This book covers the 7 bolded items out of 11 listed, which are most familiar to the consumer.

1. **Brand name**
2. **Class & type designation**
3. **Alcohol content**
4. **Name & address**
5. **Net contents**
6. **Sulfite declaration**
7. **Health warning statement**
8. FD & C yellow # 5 disclosure
9. Saccharin disclosure
10. Percentage of foreign wine
11. Country of origin

Chapter 1: Brand name

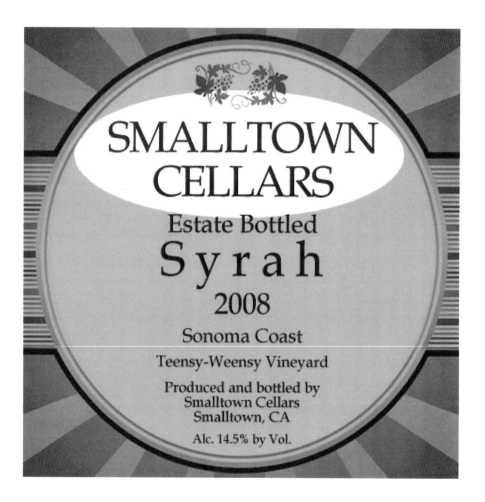

The first required item, the wine's brand name, is also the most commonly used search tool for consumers. Just like clothing, household products, or electronics, we are accustomed to shopping for wine by brand name.

In most cases, the wine's brand name is also the name of the winery. When wineries sell under what is called a *second label*, however, the wine has a different brand name and is usually sold in a lower price range. One winery may bottle wines under 5, 10 or 20 different brand names, depending on their marketing plan.

There are also many wines sold on the market today by individuals or entities that hold wholesale licenses. They fall into the industry category known as *custom crush clients or wholesalers.* These custom crush clients generally do not have their own winery, but enter into a contract agreement to have their wines made and bottled by an established winery. Custom crush operations have grown dramatically in the past decade, largely because people with a long-time passion for wine are able to get their start in the industry without making the investment of building their own winery.

The TTB places one requirement in particular on the use of brand names they cannot be "misleading". The TTB's definition of misleading for brand names is they cannot "create any impression or inference as to the age, origin, identity, or other characteristics of the product unless qualified by the word *brand* or when not so qualified, conveys no erroneous impressions as to the age, origin, identity, or other characteristics of the product."

Here are a couple of examples of using "origin" in a brand name that would be allowed provided the wine blend itself qualified for it. A brand name that includes the name of a specific vineyard or ranch must comply with the TTB's percentage requirements for the use of vineyard names. (See chapter 11) This is also the case if a brand name contains the name of an established viticultural area (AVA, see chapter 10) The TTB doesn't want any wine laying claims to specifically defined terms that it doesn't qualify for.

Primarily, a wine's brand name is tossed around in wine discussions, searched for on store shelves, and is the name consumers have come to recognize.

Favorite story:

My favorite story to share with you about brand names is one where I was assisting a custom crush client with their label design and label approval submission. The brand name they had chosen for their wine was "Que Syrah". (Can you guess the wine's varietal?) When I submitted their label for approval it came back to us with the regulation violation message that "Class & type designators cannot be used in a brand name". Translation, your brand name cannot contain a varietal name. I informed the custom crush client about this and they went back to the drawing board and came up with "Que Sera" to replace it. A clever edit and sure enough, the TTB gave the label their approval.

Chapter 2: Class and Type

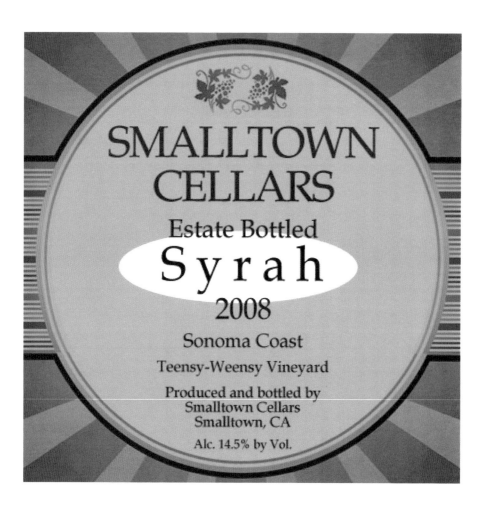

The class and type of wine is another required label item that is a commonly used consumer shopping guide. The "class" that this TTB category is referring to for the purposes of this book is called the "Grape Wine" class. This class makes up the majority of wine made in the US. Some other examples of TTB classes of wine are; sparkling, citrus and fruit. The second half of this required item, the "Type" is what refers to the wines more specific identity. The TTB's list of types currently contains a total of over 100, but most of us are familiar with the second to last one on the list titled, "single varietal wines,". (More to come about this in Chapter 8). A wine may be labeled by its grape's varietal *type*, such as Zinfandel, Sauvignon Blanc, etc. A wine may also be labeled as a *blend* of several varietal types of wine.

On the flip side of listing a varietal as your required "type" is the other end of the spectrum. An actual varietal name, such as Chardonnay, Cabernet Sauvignon, Zinfandel or Sauvignon Blanc is never required on a label. Instead you can list one of the most basic examples of required "types" of grape wine which appear at the very beginning of the TTB's type list. These three very generic identifiers are: "red wine," "white wine," and "rose wine." And what do you suppose are the requirements for using these most basic "type" names? The wine must only match the color designated. For marketing reasons, wineries may or may not prefer to use a varietal name on their label. However, if they do choose to include one, TTB regulations require that the blend have a minimum of 75% of the stated varietal in it. So when you read a wine label which bears the varietal type Syrah, (Such as our Smalltown Cellars example) you can be sure that type of grape makes up at least 75% of the wine.

On the flip side of this scenario, a consumer viewing a wine label that only states "red wine" (but no varietal name) can't know for sure what is or is not in that wine's blend. The wine could actually be 100% from just one varietal, but for marketing or pricing reasons the winery chose to label it simply "red wine."

In this case the winery will often then list details about a wine's varietal blend breakdown in the back label text, offering the consumer more detail about the varietal makeup of the wine. The TTB requires that when wine blend varietals are listed on the back label they be put in descending order, down to any varietal that accounts for at least 5% of the blend.

Here's an example of how this might look on a label: the front label on a wine may state, "Red Wine" and the back label text further describes it as a blend of Cabernet Sauvignon, Cabernet Franc, Merlot, and Petite Sirah. You as the consumer of this wine now know more intimate details about this wine which can add to your overall tasting appreciation. In general consumers can glean more intimate details about a wine blend based on whether or not it bears a varietal name on the front label or the varietal blend breakdown on the back label.

Favorite story:

I have two favorite stories to share with you from my experiences with this label item and since I couldn't decide which was better to share here I've included them both.

After starting to work at a long established winery as their compliance manager a wine they had been making for many years came up for bottling so we were taking a look at its newly designed label to see if a new label approval was needed. As part of this process I was comparing the past year's label to the current draft to see what changes had been made. A part of this label review process involves looking at the current wine blend's breakdown details to confirm what it does (Or does not) qualify to use on its label. I realized that for the past several years they had been listing the varietals in the blend on the back label, but never comparing them to the actual blend statistics and updating the label accordingly to make sure they were listed in descending order. (The blend tended to change from year to year) When I informed them of this their reaction was a very common one, they simply had no idea that those were the regulation requirements and were more than willing to make any changes necessary so the blend was accurately listed.

Favorite story #2:

I submitted a label approval for a wine that listed "*pinot noir blanc*" as the class & type on its front label. On the back label the text further described the wine as having a "ruby jewel like color". Apparently the TTB specialist viewing my label for approval had a good memory of their high school French as they sent the label back objecting to the mis-matched terms from the front to the back label. "Blanc" of course translates to "white", so the front label was stating the wine was white in color, while the back label made specific reference to the color as "ruby". To satisfy the TTB we edited the back label text to simply, "this wine has a beautiful, jewel like color" deleting any reference to an actual color and this satisfied the TTB specialist to give it their approval.

Chapter 3: Alcohol Content

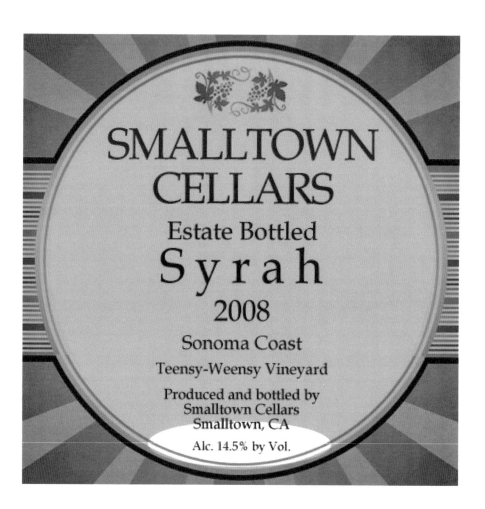

SMALLTOWN CELLARS

Estate Bottled

Syrah

2008

Sonoma Coast

Teensy-Weensy Vineyard

Produced and bottled by
Smalltown Cellars
Smalltown, CA

Alc. 14.5% by Vol.

As mentioned earlier, a tax has been placed on alcoholic beverages since the very early days of U.S. history. Between the years of 1868 to 1913 90% of the IRS's revenues came from taxes on alcohol and tobacco.

Current day wine taxation consists of two tax classes of still wine: table wine and dessert wine. The table wine tax class includes all still wines made with 7% to 14% alcohol content. Wineries pay a current federal tax rate of $1.07 per gallon for wines in the table wine tax class. The dessert wine tax class covers wines made with 14% to 21% alcohol content. The current tax rate for this class is $1.57 per gallon.

Many so-classed "dessert wines" don't seem like dessert wines to modern wine drinkers. But once upon a time, grape growing and winemaking styles were such that wines rarely had alcohols even close, let alone higher than 14% — and if they did, they were of the sherry or port style so were served at that portion of a meal.

Another aspect of alcohol content labeling is that the TTB has allowable tolerance ranges. In other words, the alcohol content number on a wine's label is allowed to vary a bit from the wines true alcohol content. For the lower table wine tax class, that tolerance range is plus or minus 1.5%, and for the higher dessert wine tax class the range is 1.0%. A key exception that wineries must pay attention to is never to "cross over" tax class lines. So, for example, if a wine has an actual alcohol of 13.2% its label alcohol could go as low as 11.7% but only as high as 14.0% (because it must still fall within the table wine limits).

As a second example, looking at our Smalltown Cellars label alcohol of 14.5% and applying the 1.0% tolerance range allowed for wines in its tax class we know the actual alcohol of this wine to be between 14.1 and 15.5%. From the perspective of a winery they want to make sure they label their wines with the appropriate alcohol and pay their federal taxes on that amount. Being familiar with the tax classes and their tolerance ranges ensures they don't either underpay or overpay.

Alcohol content statements are also often used as marketing tools to give certain impressions about a wine's character. A lower range alcohol content number will be used to give the impression of a lighter style, especially with white wines, for example.

On the other end of the alcohol spectrum for wine, many red wine producers have started using riper and riper grapes in the last decade which results in a much higher alcohol content. (Due to the roughly 2 to 1 conversion of sugar to alcohol) When it comes time to design the label for the finished product, they don't want to scare off the consumer with a high alcohol content number, so they tend to state a lower percentage on the label, using up their allowed 1.0% tolerance range. (In the dessert wine tax class)

Prior to this riper grape trend, alcohol content percentages on wine labels were much lower and they were usually formatted as either whole numbers or in increments of .5%. They were, for example, 13.0%, 13.5%, etc. If you start taking a look at current labels, you will notice that their alcohol percentages run the whole gamut of the decimal place range — you will see 13.1% 13.2%, 13.3%, 13.4%, etc. This indicates that many wineries are doing the math on tolerance ranges to see the full spectrum of numbers available to them, and are able to choose either the highest or lowest possible end of that spectrum.

You may also notice on occasion a wine label which has the term "table wine" on it. Table wine, as previously stated, is one of the tax classes of still wine, corresponding to wines with alcohols in the range of 7% to 14%. The TTB allows a winery to simply put the phrase "table wine" on their label in place of an actual alcohol content percent. This is only the case for wines in this 7% to 14% alcohol range. (Wines in the higher 14% to 21% dessert wine class are always required to have a specific alcohol content percentage on their labels.)

The TTB also accepts use of the term "light wine" for the lower range, or table wine class. However, this term is rarely used, given the confusion it would cause in our diet-focused marketplace of calorie-conscious shoppers!

Favorite story:

My favorite story to share with you about alcohol content is not so much a story as rather what has been an interesting debate to watch. That debate has been around the high level of concern over the tolerance range that wine alcohols are allowed to have. Many wine industry professionals feel that these tolerance ranges, and the wineries who take full use of them are practicing a form of false advertising. It is their opinion that wineries are deceiving their customers over a falsely low or high effect from the alcohol content in their wine. I don't tend to see any issue here myself, probably because the bulk of my first hand experiences working with wineries are that the label alcohol they choose is within .5% of the actual alcohol content of the wine. To me, with wine that's close enough.

Chapter 4: Health Warning Statement

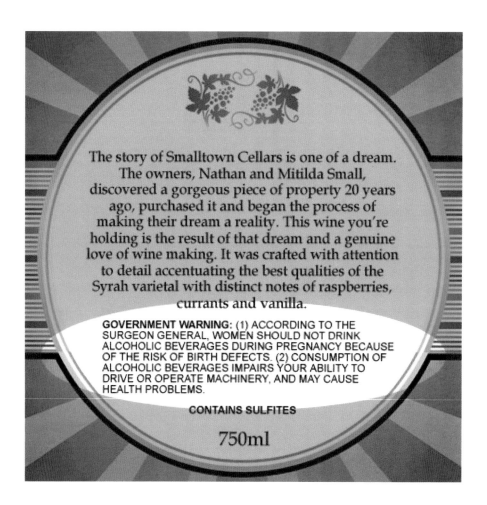

The story of Smalltown Cellars is one of a dream. The owners, Nathan and Mitilda Small, discovered a gorgeous piece of property 20 years ago, purchased it and began the process of making their dream a reality. This wine you're holding is the result of that dream and a genuine love of wine making. It was crafted with attention to detail accentuating the best qualities of the Syrah varietal with distinct notes of raspberries, currants and vanilla.

GOVERNMENT WARNING: (1) ACCORDING TO THE SURGEON GENERAL, WOMEN SHOULD NOT DRINK ALCOHOLIC BEVERAGES DURING PREGNANCY BECAUSE OF THE RISK OF BIRTH DEFECTS. (2) CONSUMPTION OF ALCOHOLIC BEVERAGES IMPAIRS YOUR ABILITY TO DRIVE OR OPERATE MACHINERY, AND MAY CAUSE HEALTH PROBLEMS.

CONTAINS SULFITES

750ml

As the old saying goes, "Things used to be a lot simpler." This surely applies to wine labels. In the interest of protecting the consumer, and in large part due to the efforts of teetotaler Senator Strom Thurmond, late in 1988 Congress ruled that a specific health warning statement be required on all alcoholic beverages containing more than 4.0% alcohol and bottled after November 18, 1989. This two sentence-long statement has several specific requirements about the health warning's font size, placement and proximity to anything else on the label. It is often the item that will cause a label to be rejected during its approval process — simply because it is missing one comma, or because other text or details on the label are "too close" to it in the eyes of the TTB specialist viewing it for approval. The next time you pick up a wine bottle take a look at this statement and notice how nothing else is nudged immediately up against it.

One of the specific requirements of this statement is that it must appear on a "contrasting background." For wine labels designed with a black background, the use of dark lettering for this statement can open up a debate with the TTB about whether or not there is enough contrast. Additional challenges can arise due to TTB's electronic version of the label approval process, introduced in 2002. This very efficient process has many advantages over the original version of sending hard copies in the mail, but it also means that labels are viewed in a digital image format, which sometimes doesn't do the hard copy justice. The TTB is very protective of this required label item, so for wineries their best practice is to adhere to their standards surrounding it.

Favorite story:

I have had a few experiences in the process of a label approval where the specialist viewing the label objected to the words "government warning" not being bold enough in their eyes or on enough of a contrasting background. In all these situations the label they were viewing was an electronic version which did not translate for viewing electronically exactly like the printed version. In each case I did some special editing myself to the electronic file and re-sent it to the TTB. Sure enough they came back approved right away. I've also seen examples of typos and other label items being "too close" to it so the label came back rejected until we fixed it.

I'm not proud to admit it, but I can recite this required wine label statement by heart, including punctuation.

Chapter 5: Name and Address

SMALLTOWN
CELLARS
Estate Bottled
Syrah
2008
Sonoma Coast
Teensy-Weensy Vineyard

Produced and bottled by
Smalltown Cellars
Smalltown, CA

Alc. 14.5% by Vol.

The TTB's terminology for number 5 on our list of required items is the "name and address statement," but it is also often referred to as the "bottler's statement." The requirements that guide this statement correspond to the winery site that physically bottled (or imported) the wine. The TTB requires this statement contain, at a bare minimum, three items:

1. The phrase "bottled by" or "imported by," whichever is applicable
2. An operating or trade name which must be identical to a name listed on the basic permit
3. The city and state of the company/winery, which must match the address listed on its original TTB permit

An example of the bare minimum requirements for this statement would be: "Bottled by XYZ Winery, Somewhere, CA." In considering the second item on our list, you may be wondering, "What is a trade name?" Trade names are any and all names that a winery plans to place in the space immediately after "bottled by" in this required statement on all wines that are bottled at its site. Sometimes, a trade name is used when wineries have a second label.

Using the example above, XYZ Winery makes wines using their winery name as the brand name, but they might also make wine under a second label, or alternative brand name, so they can sell at a lower price point. Let's say the second label is branded Hillside Cellars. The name and address statement on the label for that wine would read: "Bottled by Hillside Cellars, Somewhere, CA"

Trade names are also used in place of the actual winery name when that winery bottles wine for custom crush clients. The custom crush client must tell the winery what trade names they will use, and the winery is responsible for informing the TTB of those trade names. So, if XYZ Winery custom crushes a wine sold by Carpetbagger Wines, even if the Carpetbagger offices operate in different state, the name and address statement would read: "Bottled by Carpetbagger Wines, Somewhere, CA."

Favorite story:

My favorite insider story to share here with you is more of an insiders tip. This tip is for how you can crack the code to tell if a wine is made by a winery or a custom crush client. This is a two step process. Step one look at the "bottled by" statement on the label and locate the trade name used there. Next do a web search for that name and see what comes up. If you actually locate a website for a winery, (with a physical address & visiting information) then you have your answer. If however you find a website for wines under that trade name but it doesn't list any info about having a physical location you can actually visit this will tell you they are most likely a custom crush client type of wine business.

Chapter 6: Sulfite Statement

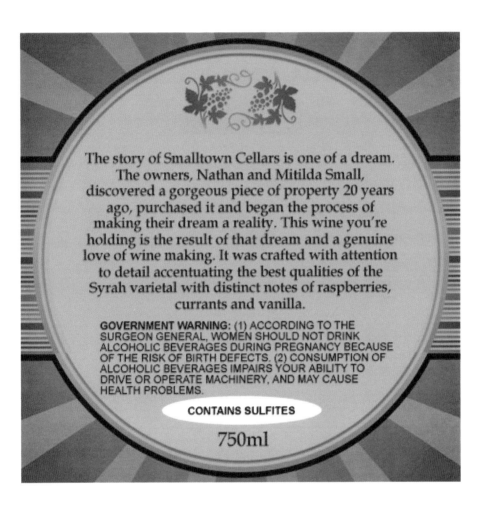

The story of Smalltown Cellars is one of a dream. The owners, Nathan and Mitilda Small, discovered a gorgeous piece of property 20 years ago, purchased it and began the process of making their dream a reality. This wine you're holding is the result of that dream and a genuine love of wine making. It was crafted with attention to detail accentuating the best qualities of the Syrah varietal with distinct notes of raspberries, currants and vanilla.

GOVERNMENT WARNING: (1) ACCORDING TO THE SURGEON GENERAL, WOMEN SHOULD NOT DRINK ALCOHOLIC BEVERAGES DURING PREGNANCY BECAUSE OF THE RISK OF BIRTH DEFECTS. (2) CONSUMPTION OF ALCOHOLIC BEVERAGES IMPAIRS YOUR ABILITY TO DRIVE OR OPERATE MACHINERY, AND MAY CAUSE HEALTH PROBLEMS.

CONTAINS SULFITES

750ml

The sulfite statement was first introduced on wine labels on January 9, 1987. It is required to appear on the label of wines with more than 10 parts per million of sulfur dioxide, which includes the vast majority of wines sold. The requirement came about in part due to the influence of the health lobby, which articulated concern over allergic sensitivities to sulfur. Sulfur dioxide is a prevalent product used in most grape growing and winemaking processes. It serves to preserve from spoilage in both situations. Sulfur dioxide is also present in the genetic make-up of wine grapes. For winemaking style or marketing purposes, some wineries specifically choose to limit their use of sulfur dioxide once the grapes have come into the winery.

If a winery chooses not to put the "Contains Sulfites" statement that is required, they must submit proof, in the form of a certified laboratory test, which documents that the total sulfur dioxide level is less than 10 parts per million. But even if a wine passes the low-sulfur lab test, the label text is not allowed to make any direct reference to the low-use or no-use of sulfur, as the TTB has determined that such statements are potentially confusing or misleading to the consumer.

Favorite story:

I submitted a label approval for a wine that qualified for not putting the "contains sulfites" statement on its label. The original back label text contained this sentence, "This wine was made without the addition of sulfur dioxide". It was sent back to us out of objection that this statement could potentially "mislead the public" into thinking there was no sulfur dioxide at all in the wine. At first we threw our hands up over an objection that came down to what seemed like subjective semantics, but rather than go through on this objection we revised that sentence to, "we chose to omit preservatives during the winemaking process" and sure enough another label became approved.

Chapter 7: Net Contents

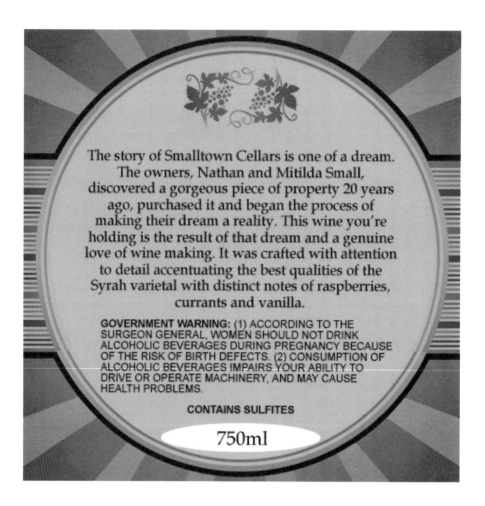

The story of Smalltown Cellars is one of a dream. The owners, Nathan and Mitilda Small, discovered a gorgeous piece of property 20 years ago, purchased it and began the process of making their dream a reality. This wine you're holding is the result of that dream and a genuine love of wine making. It was crafted with attention to detail accentuating the best qualities of the Syrah varietal with distinct notes of raspberries, currants and vanilla.

GOVERNMENT WARNING: (1) ACCORDING TO THE SURGEON GENERAL, WOMEN SHOULD NOT DRINK ALCOHOLIC BEVERAGES DURING PREGNANCY BECAUSE OF THE RISK OF BIRTH DEFECTS. (2) CONSUMPTION OF ALCOHOLIC BEVERAGES IMPAIRS YOUR ABILITY TO DRIVE OR OPERATE MACHINERY, AND MAY CAUSE HEALTH PROBLEMS.

CONTAINS SULFITES

750ml

The last of the TTB-required items being covered in this book is the net contents statement. A wine's net contents must be represented in very specific metric amounts. For example, the most common wine bottle holds 750 milliliters. This size of bottle must be marked using the term "milliliter." Using another metric equivalent of that amount, such as 75 centiliters, is not acceptable. Bottles larger than 1 liter are required to be stated in liters and in decimal portions of a liter down to the nearest hundredth. Such detail!

Because the TTB wants to ensure that the wine-buying consumer is getting their moneys worth, bottle capacity must be displayed, and here again tolerance ranges are enforced, this time in reference to fill amounts. For a 750-milliliter bottle, the fill tolerance range is 2% — or 15 milliliters. If you've examined a lot of wine bottles, you may have noticed that the amount a bottle can hold is often molded into the glass along the bottom edge of the bottle. The TTB does allow the net contents to be displayed in this way, but only if the numbers are located on the outermost surface of the bottle. Some bottle manufacturers place the net content amount into the punt of the bottle (the indentation on the bottom). That is not

TTB-compliant. The net contents regulation came into effect for all wines bottled after January 1, 1979.

Favorite story:

Most wine bottles are manufactured outside of the US. The orders for the glass are placed months ahead of when the wine will be bottled. I've submitted many label approvals where we indicated that the net contents of "750 ml" was "blown into glass" as in my description the TTB allows from above. However what happened on more than one occasion was when the actual glass shipment arrived sure enough there it was, not "750 ml" on the bottom outside of the bottles, but "75 cl" hiding inside the punt. This was especially the case for glass that came from European factories I suppose the Europeans are more partial to centiliters than milliliters when it comes to their wines.

Information *Not* Required on Wine Labels

Many of the elements seen on wine labels are actually not required to be there. Though the TTB does not require the 7 items listed below, it does regulate them if they are included. For example, if a certain item is on the label, it may automatically require the inclusion of another item on the list. And, for some items on this non-required list, specific percentage requirements must be met and/or other details must be included. Some of these non-required pieces of information are seen as quality indicators while others reveal different aspects of the wine's story.

The 7 most common non-TTB-required items to appear on wine labels are:

1. Varietal
2. Vintage
3. Appellation
4. Vineyard designate
5. Optional name and address statements

6. Estate bottled

7. Funny, factual, or flowery back label text

Does it look like all of this is starting to get a bit complicated and intertwined? That is certainly the case — especially the more detailed a wine label gets. But as you become more familiar with wine label informational items you as the savvy consumer then get to enjoy the insider details about any wine you pick up.

Reading through this list you may be surprised to see many items we're very used to seeing on wine labels, and perhaps even commonly relying on them as purchasing guides of sorts. (Think, "I'm looking for a Napa Valley Cabernet")

Wineries don't just know this about you their customer but they use these identifiers because they take definite pride in them about their wines so naturally they are inclined to display them on their wine's label.

Chapter 8: Varietal

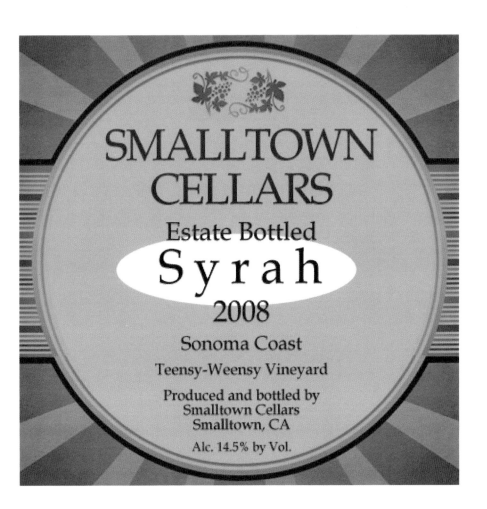

SMALLTOWN
CELLARS
Estate Bottled
Syrah
2008
Sonoma Coast
Teensy-Weensy Vineyard
Produced and bottled by
Smalltown Cellars
Smalltown, CA
Alc. 14.5% by Vol.

Chapter 2, Class and Type, touched on the subject of varietals. Some sort of class and type specification is always required on a wine label, and while a varietal name is an example of such a specification, it is not actually required to be used.

However, a varietal name is another very common search topic for wine consumers as they grow to prefer specific varietals of wine. As stated previously, the TTB's varietal label regulations require that a blend be made up of at least 75% of the stated varietal to use it on its label.

Wineries also have the option of placing more than one varietal on a front label. Two or more varietals can be listed there, and in that case the percentages of each must also appear next to them with their total adding up to 100%.

As was discussed in chapter 2, wineries also have the option of naming a single varietal on their front label and then listing it along with the other varietals in the blend on the back label. In this case, they do not need to list all of the percentage information, but they do need to list the varietals in descending order, down to any varietal that accounts for at least 5% of the blend.

Use of a varietal on a wine label is our first example of an item which if used automatically requires the use of another non-required item: an appellation of origin. The two are directly connected; the TTB requires that at least 75% of the fruit used to make up the 75% minimum of the stated varietal must be from the appellation indicated.

So for our Smalltown Cellars label here with a varietal of Syrah and an appellation of Sonoma Coast we know that this wine contains at least 75% Syrah sourced from the Sonoma Coast appellation. As wine consumers we are accustomed to viewing a generally small range of varietal names on the wines we buy. The actual list of grape names approved for use on labels on the TTB's site currently lists over 250 varietals.

Favorite story:

I've seen a lot of wine labels over my years interacting with wineries, but one came along that caught me off guard with its varietal details vs. its "type". First, this is what it listed on the front label as its "type": Red Table Wine. Sure, nothing unusual about that. But then to give their customers some additional intimate details about the wine they also chose to list the varietals and their percentages and this is what threw me a bit. The varietal breakdown was this: "Viognier 89%, Syrah 5%, Carignane 5%, & Grenache 1%". Viognier is a white grape and the next three varietals listed here are all red grapes, so at 89% Viognier, I was asking, where did the "Red" come from? The answer came from the winemaking description on the back label, but I offer this story as an example of the wide range of creativity that wineries and wine brand owners often put into the design of their labels. Some that even stump us label vets!

Chapter 9: Vintage

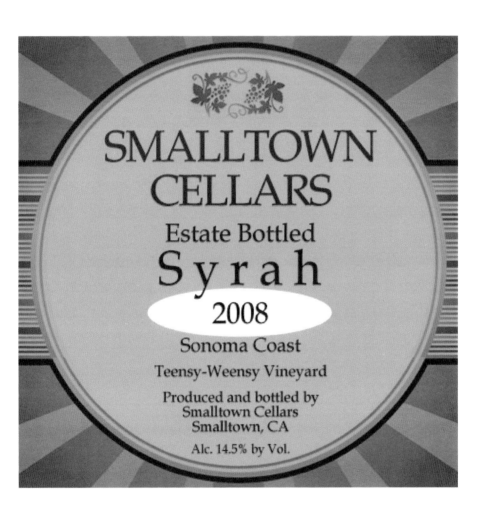

SMALLTOWN
CELLARS
Estate Bottled
Syrah
2008
Sonoma Coast
Teensy-Weensy Vineyard
Produced and bottled by
Smalltown Cellars
Smalltown, CA
Alc. 14.5% by Vol.

What vintage is that wine? This has long been another way of asking what year (or age) the wine is. Though a vintage date is commonly seen on wine labels, it is not required by the TTB.

When wineries do choose to include vintage information on their label here again like the use of a varietal, an appellation is also required. In fact, there are also two categories of minimum percentage requirements when a vintage is listed which correspond directly to the type of appellation used.

The first category for minimum percentage requirements is if the appellation is an American viticultural area, or AVA. AVAs are specifically defined geographic areas approved by the TTB with distinctive growing conditions and historical data unique to the region. If an AVA is used on a label, the vintage requirements are a minimum of 95%. This means that 95% of the grapes used to make the wine must have been harvested in that year.

The second category for appellation designation is if a political subdivision is used, such as a county name or state name. In this case, the vintage requirements are a minimum of 85%.

So, if a wine's label states, "Russian River Valley," (an AVA) as its appellation along with "2008" as its vintage that would mean that at least 95% of the blend came from fruit harvested in the 2008 season. BUT. it doesn't mean that 95% of the fruit came from the Russian River Valley AVA! Only 85% of the fruit must have come from that AVA (we'll get into this in the next chapter). Likewise, a label stating an appellation of, "Mendocino County" and "2008" would indicate that at least 85% of the blend consists of fruit harvested in the 2008 season. This wider range for wines listing a political subdivision as their appellation came into effect in 2006 as a result of the industry lobbying to congress to update the TTB regulations. Prior to that the vintage percentage requirement had been 95% across the board which was a challenge for many wineries to accommodate due to the fact that several vintages of wine live on their sites throughout the year and are accessed come final blending time for bottling.

Chapter 10: Appellation

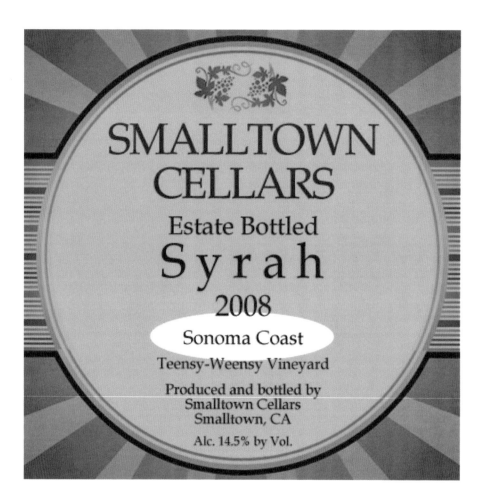

SMALLTOWN
CELLARS
Estate Bottled
S y r a h
2008
Sonoma Coast
Teensy-Weensy Vineyard
Produced and bottled by
Smalltown Cellars
Smalltown, CA
Alc. 14.5% by Vol.

Like the importance of location, location, location in the real estate market, the wine world places significant value on the source of the grapes used to make the wine. As referred to in the previous chapter, there are two types of appellations seen on wine labels: American viticultural areas (or AVAs) and political subdivisions.

An AVA is a designated geographic area which has been approved by the TTB and is noted for its characteristics related to soil, climate and overall growing conditions that make it well suited to growing certain grape varietals and producing wines with certain characteristics. All AVAs are appellations. When using an AVA on a wine label the minimum percentage requirement is 85%, meaning 85% of the wine must be made from grapes grown in that AVA.

Appellations of origin that are **not** AVAs are political subdivision appellations. Sonoma County, Washington and New York are all examples of political subdivisions. When using a political subdivision on a wine label the minimum percentage requirement is 75%, meaning 75% of the wine must be made from grapes grown in that political subdivision.

An appellation can be a marketing tool. Because well-known and desirable wine grapes are grown in specific AVAs (such as Napa Valley, Russian River Valley, etc.), having that AVA on your wine label implies a level of quality to the consumer. Of course some AVA names won't look familiar to consumers so it has become a common trend for the county name to be put immediately below the AVA name on a label. This is to assist the consumer in knowing where the grapes were grown. And though these labels do list two appellations on them (the AVA and the county name), the wine is still required to meet the stricter minimum percentage required for listing an AVA (85%) on the label.

As an example, a wine label may list the AVA "Alexander Valley" and then list below it "Sonoma County," since Sonoma County is recognized by most consumers and "Alexander Valley" may not be.

There are currently 207 AVAs in the U.S. and over 50% of those are in California. So you can see why the wineries might decide to put both types of appellation on their labels to assist their customers make the place connection when viewing them.

Favorite story:

My favorite insider's story to share with you about AVAs is in regards to the saga around the approval process of the Calistoga AVA in 2009. Normally the AVA application and approval process takes a matter of months to happen. For a period from 2006 til 2009 we were seeing new AVAs approved on what seemed like a weekly basis. So then in 2005 when I saw that a petition had been submitted for a Calistoga AVA I fully expected it to be added to their official list by year's end. (I also thought "about time!") Months turned into years as this AVA was objected to by two Calistoga wineries that had "Calistoga" in their actual winery name. They were objecting to the impact approving this AVA would have on their future labels. (Use of an AVA name in a brand name would only be allowed if the wine blend always qualified for the percentage requirements for AVA.) Both of these wineries with Calistoga in their name sourced the majority of their fruit from outside of the proposed AVA boundaries. Senator Mike Thompson even got involved on this one and in late 2009, it was officially approved.

Chapter 11: Vineyard Designate

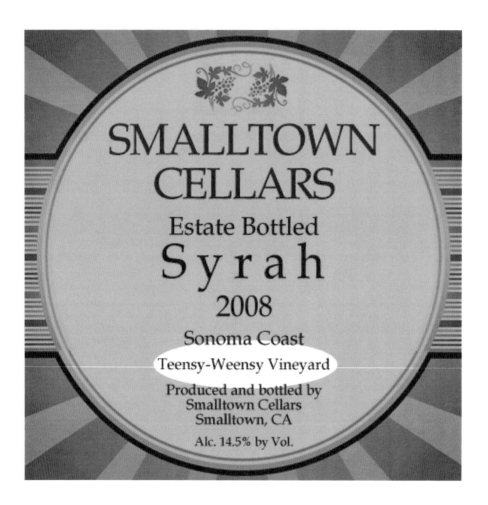

SMALLTOWN CELLARS

Estate Bottled

Syrah

2008

Sonoma Coast

Teensy-Weensy Vineyard

Produced and bottled by
Smalltown Cellars
Smalltown, CA

Alc. 14.5% by Vol.

This next item often seen on wine labels is what is called a vineyard designate, which is the term for a specific vineyard name listed on the label. When a winery chooses to include the name of the vineyard, farm or ranch from which the grapes used to make the wine were grown, the minimum required percentage, per TTB regulations, is 95%. The details on these regulations go deeper.

The winery's records must show the wine's connection to the original vineyard name across the life of the wine, from grape to processing to bottling. Of course the use of a vineyard name is yet another marketing tool with implications of a higher quality level. Consumers associate the appearance of a single vineyard name with purity. Those who really pay attention may begin to notice certain vineyard names appearing on labels from multiple wineries, because grape growers often have relationships with multiple wine producers. The savvy consumer can potentially use vineyard designate labeling, like varietal and appellation labeling, as another shopping guide, developing preferences for certain characteristics related to the certain vineyards with which they become familiar.

A brand name does not a vineyard designate make. Buyer beware! Though it is commonplace to use the word "Vineyard" as part of a brand name on a wine label this does not imply a vineyard designate. Many wineries have the word "vineyard" in their company name. Beringer Vineyards, for example, is the name of a wine brand, (And winery) but not the vineyard used as a source of fruit. And as a consumer, you can easily spot the difference between brand and vineyard designate by the placement and size of each on the label. In the case of our Smalltown Cellars label Smalltown Cellars is the brand name and Teensy-Weensy Vineyard is the vineyard designate.

Favorite story:

As was referred to earlier the use of all wine label items requires specific recordkeeping maintenance that document qualifying for their use. In the case of displaying a vineyard name on a wine label the winery would need to document it with that specific vineyard name starting with its beginning record keeping document, which in the case of wine grapes is a form called a weigh tag.

At one of the wineries where I managed winemaking records we were coming up on the bottling date for a wine we would be bottling for the first time. The blend, at over 95% from one vineyard site qualified to list a vineyard designate on its label.

Problem was the vineyard name we had listed on all of the weigh tags for the grapes and other winemaking records was not the one the winemaker had now decided he'd like to call it on the label. The vineyard site had previously always been called just the property owners last name. However since this was a newly created wine the winemaker wanted to give it a more original name as well. What did this mean for our recordkeeping? To comply with the TTB's regulations we had to trace back into all of our records for the wine blend throughout its life and edit them to display the newly created vineyard name, starting with the weigh tags and coming forward up through the soon to be bottling records. Fortunately this was not a very large wine blend so accomplishing this records re-do was not a terribly daunting task.

Chapter 12: Optional Name and Address Statements

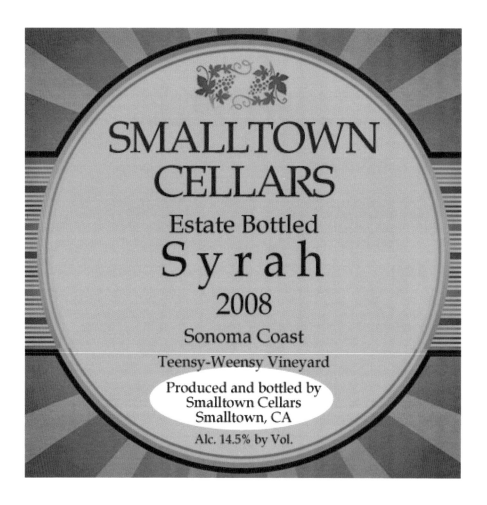

As we've already established, all U.S. wine labels are required to have the minimum statement of "Bottled by [Name of Winery/Trade Name], [City], [State]." Consumers who spend time looking at labels, however will notice additional terminology in most bottler's statements. The TTB provides a specific list of what are called "optional" statements, which have defined requirements that must be met for their use. There are 6 optional phrases available for wineries to clarify their bottler's statements. These options are always placed before the words "Bottled by."

The 6 optional phrases are:

Blended
Cellared
Produced
Made
Prepared
Vinted

Each of these phrases has a specific definition, with some being more involved than others. Here are their definitions:

Blended means that the winery "mixed the wine with other wines of the same class and type." This means a winery has put together (blended) at least two different wines to make the final wine that went into the bottle. It could have been a much more involved process than that, but at a minimum, that is what would have been required.

Cellared means that the winery "subjected the wine to cellar treatment." There is a detailed list of what the TTB accepts as cellar treatments, and these range from very basic chemical additions to more involved processes such as filtration. If this phrase is seen on a wine label, it usually means that the winery that bottled the wine didn't actually "make" the wine. See the next paragraph for more clarification.

Produced means that the bottling winery "fermented not less than 75% of the wine." This is the only optional phrase where minimum percentage requirements come into play. It used to be common practice for wineries to make and bottle all their wines on the same site. But in the last 20 years of industry development, two trends have emerged:

1. Many wineries have more than one physical site where their wines are made.

2. Wineries regularly buy and sell wines from and to the bulk market.

Both of these trends have created the need for greater specificity on wine labels.

Made has the same definition as *produced*, so it, too, requires that a 75% minimum of the wine blend must have been fermented at the site where the wine was bottled.

Prepared and *vinted* have the same requirements as *cellared*. The winery must have subjected the wine to cellar treatment in order to employ these terms on the label.

Generally, when the phrases *blended*, *cellared*, *prepared*, or *vinted* are seen on a wine label, that is code for, "This majority of this wine was made at a winery site other than the one where it was bottled." Of those four optional phrases, the most commonly used are *cellared* and *vinted*. From a marketing standpoint, the phrase *produced* is always desirable if a wine qualifies for it. Many wineries have a strong dislike for any of the other terms besides *produced,* so if they did not ferment the minimum amount of wine to qualify for it, they will just leave the statement at its bare minimum requirement of "bottled by." Of all the optional statements, only *produced* and *made* require that specific percentages must be met and detailed records must be kept about the life of the wine. Though these factors may not necessarily determine how a wine tastes, they indicate a level of care and quality that is often appreciated by consumers.

Favorite story:

I've been amused on several occasions when it comes to this part of a wine's label and the strong feelings a winemaker or brand owner will have about what their options are in the event they didn't qualify for "produced". Basically their attitude was, "produced or nothing". So if their wine did not meet the minimum 75% requirement for use of "produced" in this statement then rather than select from one of the 5 other options on the list they went straight to the bare minimum statement of "bottled by". Basically they would take an "all or nothing at all" attitude. My thought in situations like this was how many of their customers were even aware of what this term even meant? (Let alone basing a purchase decision upon it!)

Chapter 13: Estate Bottled

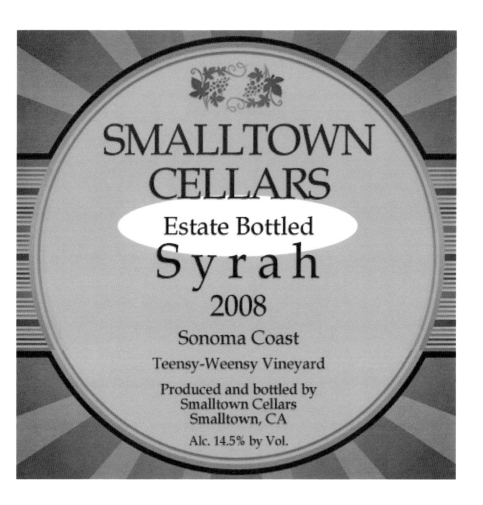

SMALLTOWN CELLARS

Estate Bottled

Syrah

2008

Sonoma Coast

Teensy-Weensy Vineyard

Produced and bottled by
Smalltown Cellars
Smalltown, CA

Alc. 14.5% by Vol.

The term *estate bottled* on a wine label indicates the "purest of the pure," or as close to a pedigree as a wine can get. Using this term on a label requires that the following Federal regulations be met:

"The term Estate Bottled may be used by a bottling winery on a wine label only if the wine is labeled with a viticultural area appellation of origin **and** the bottling winery:

1. Is located in the labeled viticultural area;

2. Grew all of the grapes used to make the wine on land owned or controlled by the winery within the boundaries of the labeled viticultural area;

3. Crushed the grapes, fermented the resulting must, and finished, aged and bottled the wine in a continuous process (the wine at no time having left the premises of the bottling winery).

4. The definition of "controlled" is: "refers to property on which the bottling winery has the legal right to perform, and does perform, all of the acts common to viticulture under the terms of a lease or similar agreement of at least 3 years duration."

So what does all that mean to a wine consumer? When a wine label states *estate bottled*, the winery grew all the grapes used to make the wine on their own vineyard property (or on vineyard property they manage in a lease of at least 3 years). They processed the wine from start to finish (from grape to bottle) at the winery site, and no part of the wine blend left the winery at any time during that process. A label that uses this term is required to also use an approved viticultural area on it as its appellation of origin, and the winery and all grapes used in the wine blend must also be in that same AVA.

For most smaller wineries which have been established for some time, meeting these requirements isn't an issue, because they have just one winery location and grow their own fruit. For medium and larger wineries to use this narrowly defined term on a label, they have to keep a close eye on the wine throughout its life to ensure that it stays "pure."

Another common term on wine labels that is similar to *estate bottled* is the term *estate grown*. The two are not the same. *Estate bottled* has its very specific definition and requirements, while *estate grown* is actually not even listed in the TTB's regulations. However, the TTB does have a regulation that applies to the second word in the phrase. To use the term "grown," all of the grapes must have been grown on land owned or controlled (for a minimum of 3 years) by the bottling winery.

Both "estate" terms are definite marketing jewels. They both put the wine into a "select" group, simply by use of the term *estate*, which connotates class and quality. A consumer need not be aware of the actual definitions behind either of the estate terms to automatically have an impression of higher quality about the wine.

Favorite story:

With use of this statement I think it is a safe statement to say that many wineries are using it while not being aware of the specific requirements behind it. This goes back to part of one of the stories I shared earlier where the winery staff was not aware of the specific TTB regulations surrounding the use of certain label terms. It has been my experience over the years with many wineries that there isn't a specific staff person keeping the close tabs on their wine's histories who is also well versed enough in the TTB's requirements to make that connection come label design time. In the case of Estate Bottled, since it is the most detailed label item unless they are a smaller winery that also grows all its own fruit, keeping up with the qualifying details and tracking whether or not a wine meets them becomes a much more involved task.

Chapter 14: Flowery, Funny or Factual Text

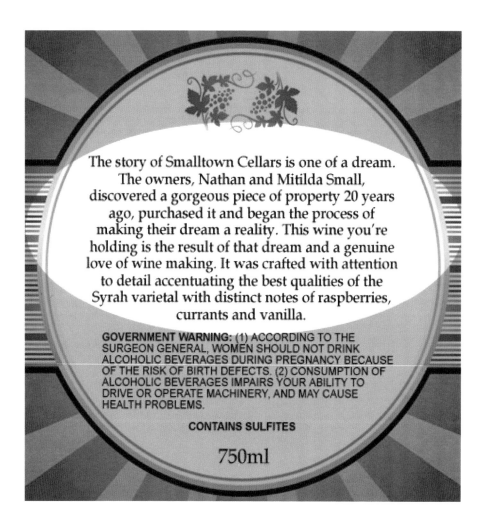

The story of Smalltown Cellars is one of a dream. The owners, Nathan and Mitilda Small, discovered a gorgeous piece of property 20 years ago, purchased it and began the process of making their dream a reality. This wine you're holding is the result of that dream and a genuine love of wine making. It was crafted with attention to detail accentuating the best qualities of the Syrah varietal with distinct notes of raspberries, currants and vanilla.

GOVERNMENT WARNING: (1) ACCORDING TO THE SURGEON GENERAL, WOMEN SHOULD NOT DRINK ALCOHOLIC BEVERAGES DURING PREGNANCY BECAUSE OF THE RISK OF BIRTH DEFECTS. (2) CONSUMPTION OF ALCOHOLIC BEVERAGES IMPAIRS YOUR ABILITY TO DRIVE OR OPERATE MACHINERY, AND MAY CAUSE HEALTH PROBLEMS.

CONTAINS SULFITES

750ml

The text on the back of a wine bottle is rarely going to incite a purchasing decision, but it can often serve as more in depth information or pure entertainment. The TTB does scrutinize all back label text and does publish a set of "general requirements" and a set of prohibited practices.

The general requirements of back label text are:

• must be legible
• must be in English (all mandatory information)
• must be truthful, accurate and specific
• must not be disparaging nor misleading

Don't those items (certainly the last two) sound like advertising requirements you'd like for any product you buy? Wineries are held accountable for these standards, and can be denied label approval if they are not met. If the back label text describes when the fruit was harvested, how long the wine was aged in barrels, or details about activities that occurred during the wine's life, those descriptions must be truthful, accurate and specific. For example, if a label states, "This wine was harvested on September 20th, from a vineyard with a 3.0 ton per acre yield," then the winery would need to ensure that they have detailed records in their files to back up those claims.

If a winery uses misleading terms on their back label such as "lively" (if the wine they are bottling is a still wine), the TTB may stop the presses, as this term is viewed as too similar to terms designated specifically for sparkling wines. The term "dessert" cannot be used on wines that have alcohol contents lower than 14%, because the TTB defines dessert wines as those with an alcohol content above 14% and up to 24%. Wineries can become quite frustrated with what can seem like nit-picky, arbitrary responses from the TTB about terms seen as "misleading." In true government speak here is the actual paragraph from the TTB regulations that is supposed to clarify for wineries what kinds of statements they cannot use.

"...Any statement that is false or untrue in any particular, or that, irrespective of falsity, directly, or by ambiguity, omission, or inference, or by the addition of irrelevant, scientific or technical matter, tends to create a misleading impression."

Clear as mud, eh?

The following is a list of prohibited practices, or items not allowed to appear on wine labels according to the TTB:

- any false or untrue statements

- any disparaging statements about competitors

- any statement or design that is obscene or indecent

- any statement, design or device or representation which tends to create the impression that a wine has intoxicating qualities

That last one is *definitely* one of the most amusing lines in the dry pages of TTB regulations. Wine not intoxicating? What do they mean by that? Their use of this term in this instance is meant to eliminate statements such as, "This wine will uplift your spirits," or "Take you to a magical place," etc. The TTB is saying it's not fair using statements that imply a wine has special magical qualities no matter how proud of it a winery may be.

Chapter 15: A Behind The Scenes Look At Wine Label Design And Approval, Start To Finish

This book has been all about taking you on a guided tour of the items you view on wine labels. To further supplement that tour now that we've covered all those items I'd like to offer you one last insider's view of the multi step process that occurs leading up to you the consumer picking a bottle off the store shelf. This is meant to be a general overview of the steps that occur, and the range of parties involved. Keep in mind that the process does vary from winery to winery depending on their staffing, and how organized (or not) they are.

Step 1:   Label design: The parties involved.

This can be a mix of many people ranging from the owner, winemaker, compliance person, marketing staff & bottling manager just to name a few. This combination of people each put in their input about what they want the label to have on it. They are deciding on everything from colors and images to each item and its location on the front and back label. From a compliance perspective here is where they are providing guidance to the others on which items (Described in this book) a wine blend qualifies to use on its label, as well as where they must be located. (Certain items must appear on the front label.)

Step 2:   Coordination with bottling schedule

The design process of a wine label also has to be coordinated well ahead of other dates, specifically the date labels will be printed and the date the wine will be bottled. Ideally in a perfect world wineries want to stick to these schedules as not doing so is a costly result. This generally means planning ahead by many months. However despite their best planning, a still very common occurrence is that wine is bottled as "shiners", meaning without labels because the labels weren't ready for one reason or another. This means extra work for the winery because they have to process those bottles twice by running them through the bottling line again when the labels do arrive.

Step 3:   Drafts…Round 1…Round 2……

Once all the parties involved in the initial design process have put in their two cents worth in Step 1 above and the initial draft of the label has been created by the printer (another party in the process) then that first draft comes back to be viewed by everybody to make sure everything is accurate, looks right, is spelled correctly, etc. More edits are made then sent back over to the printer and then back comes draft #2 for review. This process continues until all parties involved in the process give the sign off on the final draft.

Step 4:   Submit for TTB label approval

The person that submits for label approvals varies from winery to winery. Ideally they need to be someone with a good level of familiarity with TTB regulations around wine labels, unfortunately this often is not the case. As you saw from the stories I shared with you in this book there are a wide number of items that the TTB may object to in the label approval process, so ideally you want someone who is aware of what these might be to then factor into the earlier editing stage of the process. Having this knowledge will save them time, which is something they are often short on at this stage in their bottling planning as they forgot to plan ahead for the label approval step.

I'd like to add one last comment about the TTB label approval process and the items that come up as objections in their review process. The review process is largely a subjective one, as it is an individual reviewing an individual label. So what one person views as objectionable on a wine label may not be viewed the same by the next TTB staff member. This unpredictable variable to the label approval process is one that continues to frustrate those of us in the wine industry that are submitting labels for approval. Just ask anyone you know who works at a winery if they are involved in label approvals and I guarantee you'll get some sort of eye-rolling response back. Going through these sort of back and forth interactions to get your wine labels approved actually becomes sort of a feather in the cap for those of us that have dealt with many over the years. We've earned our "TTB Label Approval" badge.

There is so much going on behind the scenes that goes into a bottle of wine making its way to your store shelf and dinner table, and I find most are surprised to hear about it all. This book has been written to illuminate both industry outsiders and insiders as to all that lives on a wine label and all that goes on behind the scenes that creates what you see there. I genuinely hope you'll never look at a wine label the same way again.

In Closing

I hope the information in this book has quenched your thirst for wine label knowledge, and that you'll enjoy new insights as you pick up each bottle. I also hope the record-keeping challenges wineries face have been somewhat illuminated.

One of the most common and most satisfying responses I get from explaining this material is, "I had no idea there was so much involved!" It's quite fun to watch people take a more interactive approach to wine once they've taken the time to investigate **The Inside Story of a Wine Label.**

Should you have further questions about wine label compliance or any of the other areas of winemaking compliance, or if you'd like me to present information to your business or organization, please feel free to contact me at: ann@winecompliancealliance.com

Additional Suggested Resources

For those interested in a deeper understanding of wine and wine label compliance, here are a two websites and a book I recommend:

Websites

http://www.wineinstitute.org — The Wine Institute is the largest lobbying group for the wine industry. Their site has comprehensive lists of AVAs as well as an interesting mix of wine industry statistics.

http://www.ttb.gov/wine/wine-labeling.shtml This is the TTB's webpage dedicated to all topics related to wine labels. It provides a lot of information for industry members and consumers.

Book

From Demon to Darling: A Legal History of Wine in America

by Richard Mendelson

About Ann Reynolds

From tasting rooms to winery laboratories, from cellar work to record keeping, Ann has worked in almost every aspect of the wine industry. Her rich, 20-year plus background in winemaking informs her present work as a winemaking compliance expert and educator. Since 2006, she has taught a variety of college courses in compliance that have assisted new and veteran wine industry professionals to improve their winemaking compliance systems.

Raised in the Napa Valley of California, where she continues to live to this day, Ann has established herself as the premiere expert in winemaking compliance, from licensing and recordkeeping to labels and reporting.. She offers courses at Napa Valley College, and UC Davis when she's not helping wineries develop their winemaking compliance systems.

For more information about Ann and her services, please visit:

http://www.winecompliancealliance.com

16596394R00041

Made in the USA
Charleston, SC
30 December 2012